INDEPENDENCE HALL

All About the American Symbol

by Jessica Gunderson

PEBBLE
a capstone imprint

Pebble Explore is published by Pebble, an imprint of Capstone.
1710 Roe Crest Drive
North Mankato, Minnesota 56003
www.capstonepub.com

The name of the Smithsonian Institution and the sunburst logo are registered trademarks of the Smithsonian Institution. For more information, please visit www.si.edu.

Library of Congress Cataloging-in-Publication Data is available on the Library of Congress website.
ISBN 978-1-9771-2586-6 (library binding)
ISBN 978-1-9771-2606-1 (eBook PDF)

Summary: The site of not only the signing of the Declaration of Independence but also the signing of the U.S. Constitution, Independence Hall could not be more appropriately named. Engaging facts and photos give young report writers a comprehensive tour of this American symbol, from early building blueprints to its relevance in today's world.

Image Credits
AP Photo: 22; Architect of the Capitol: 16; Granger: 9; Library of Congress: 6–7, 11, 14, 21, Photographs in the Carol M. Highsmith Archive, 5; National Archives and Records Administration: 17; National Park Service: Independence National Historical Park, 1, 23, 25, 26, 27; North Wind Picture Archives: 13, 15; Shutterstock: Andrew J. Simcox, 24, dibrova, cover, f11photo, 29, Inspired By Maps, 18–19, ket-le (banner), back cover and throughout, Luciano Mortula LGM, 4; XNR Productions, 8

Editorial Credits
Editor: Jill Kalz; Designer: Juliette Peters; Media Researcher: Svetlana Zhurkin; Production Specialist: Laura Manthe

Our very special thanks to Kealy Gordon, Product Development Manager; Paige Towler; and the following at Smithsonian Enterprises: Jill Corcoran, Director, Licensed Publishing; Brigid Ferraro, Vice President, Consumer and Education Products; and Carol LeBlanc, President, Smithsonian Enterprises.

All internet sites appearing in back matter were available and accurate when this book was sent to press.

Printed in the United States of America.
PA117

Table of Contents

Introduction 4

The State House 6

We Want Freedom! 12

Birth of a Nation 16

A New Name 18

More Changes 20

The Hall Today 24

A Worldwide Symbol 28

Glossary 30

Read More 31

Internet Sites 31

Index 32

Words in **bold** are in the glossary.

Introduction

The United States of America has many **symbols**. Our flag is one of them. So is the Statue of Liberty. They are objects that stand for our country. **Independence** Hall is also one of those symbols.

Independence Hall is in Philadelphia, Pennsylvania. Our nation's first leaders signed an important **document** there. It was called the Declaration of Independence. It said the United States was a free country. The signing turned the brick building into a symbol of the new nation.

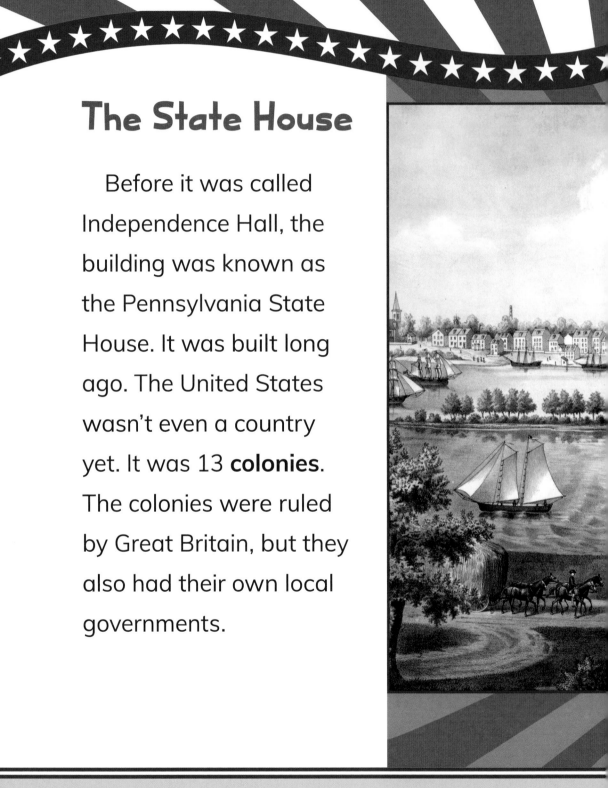

The State House

Before it was called Independence Hall, the building was known as the Pennsylvania State House. It was built long ago. The United States wasn't even a country yet. It was 13 **colonies**. The colonies were ruled by Great Britain, but they also had their own local governments.

Philadelphia, Pennsylvania
Colony, 1700–1750

In the early 1700s, colonial leaders met in one another's homes. It could be hard to travel far distances and go from place to place. Leaders needed one fixed meeting spot. Those in the colony of Pennsylvania chose Philadelphia as their spot. They had the State House built there.

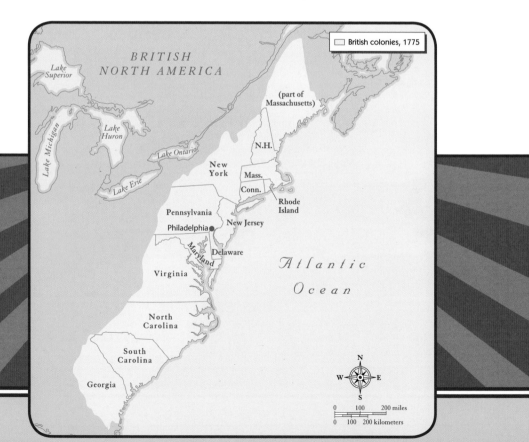

British colonies, 1775

BRITISH NORTH AMERICA

Lake Superior
Lake Michigan
Lake Huron
Lake Ontario
Lake Erie

(part of Massachusetts)

N.H.
New York
Mass.
Conn.
Rhode Island
Pennsylvania
Philadelphia
New Jersey
Maryland
Delaware
Virginia
North Carolina
South Carolina
Georgia

Atlantic Ocean

N
W E
S

0   100   200 miles
0 100 200 kilometers

Work began in 1732. The large
brick building looked neat and
balanced. Its many windows were
the same size and equally spaced.
A smaller building, called a wing,
was connected on each side.

Colonial leaders began meeting inside the State House in 1735. The second floor wasn't even finished yet! It wouldn't be finished until 1753.

At first, the building had neither a tower nor a steeple. These were added around 1750. The new structure rose high above the street. A large metal bell hung inside. It was rung to call leaders to meetings. A ringing bell also meant there was news that colonists needed to hear.

THE STATE HOUSE

We Want Freedom!

By the time the State House was finished, many colonists were unhappy with British rule.

Things got worse in 1765. British leaders needed money for their country's war against France. To get it, they made the colonists pay **taxes** on goods and paper. The colonists said this was unfair. Why should they pay taxes to a government in which they had no say?

Colonists met to talk about the unfairness of Great Britain's taxes.

The colonists decided they would no longer obey British rule. They wanted to be free. In 1774, they formed one government for all the colonies. It was called the Continental Congress.

The colonists' actions angered British leaders. Great Britain wasn't going to let the colonies go. It tried to force the colonists to obey. But the colonists fought back, and the Revolutionary War (1775–1783) began.

British soldiers (shown in red) fighting the colonists during the Revolutionary War

The Continental Congress leaving the State House on July 4, 1776

The Continental Congress met at the Pennsylvania State House. They approved the Declaration of Independence on July 4, 1776. The document said the colonies no longer belonged to Great Britain. The colonies together were a free country.

The Pennsylvania State House had become the birthplace of the United States of America.

Birth of a Nation

The Revolutionary War ended in 1783. The colonies won and were now a new nation.

As the country grew, it needed new laws. In 1787, the Continental Congress met at the State House again. This meeting was called the Constitutional Convention.

Members shared ideas. They argued. Once everyone agreed, the new laws were written down as the U.S. **Constitution**. We follow the document to this day.

A New Name

The State House got a name change in 1824, when a Revolutionary War hero visited. He was shown the **Assembly** Room. This was where the Declaration of Independence and the U.S. Constitution were signed.

From that visit on, people called the room the "hall of independence." The name stuck. Soon, the whole building was known as Independence Hall.

The Assembly Room
in Independence Hall

More Changes

The name change was just one of many changes for Independence Hall. In 1812, the building's wings had been rebuilt. Nearly 90 years later, the wings were rebuilt again.

The first wooden steeple had rotted by 1773. A new one was built in 1828. It looked fancier than the first one. A clock was added too.

In 1948, everything inside the building was redone. It was made to look like it had in the 1700s.

Independence Hall in 1876

Liberty Bell Pavilion

Independence Hall

The United States celebrated its 200th birthday in 1976. People from around the world visited Philadelphia. After all, it was the nation's birthplace.

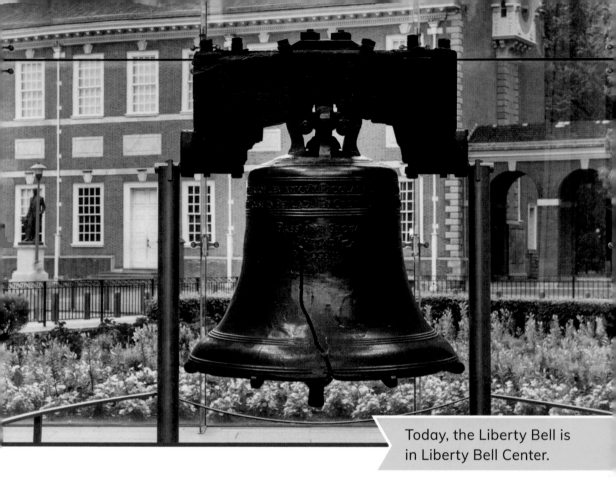

Today, the Liberty Bell is in Liberty Bell Center.

The metal bell that once hung in Independence Hall was called the Liberty Bell. Months before the nation's 200th birthday, workers moved it to a special glass shelter outside. The new spot made it easier for large crowds of people to see the bell.

The Hall Today

Today, Independence Hall is part of Independence National Historical Park. The park is about as big as 40 football fields. More than 4 million people visited it in 2019.

All the park's buildings help tell a story. They include the nation's first banks, a church, and a few homes. They tell how the United States got its start.

The First Bank of the United States

A printed copy of the Declaration of Independence is inside Independence Hall. So is a printed copy of the U.S. Constitution. The silver inkstand used to sign both documents is too.

The Assembly Room looks like it did during the Constitutional Convention. People can see and feel what it was like to be there in 1787.

A Worldwide Symbol

Independence Hall has a special place in U.S. history. It is the birthplace of our nation. It is a symbol of freedom and **democracy**. What happened inside the building is important to our country. But it is also important to many other nations around the world. Independence Hall was named a **World Heritage site** in 1979. That means it has value for people everywhere. It's a symbol to share!

Glossary

assembly (uh-SEM-blee)—a meeting of lots of people

colony (KAH-luh-nee)—an area that has been settled by people from another country; a colony is ruled by another country

constitution (kahn-stuh-TOO-shuhn)—the system of laws that state the rights of the people and the powers of the government

democracy (di-MAH-kruh-see)—a form of government in which the people can choose their leaders

document (DAHK-you-muhnt)—a piece of paper that contains important information

independence (IN-dee-PEN-denss)—freedom

symbol (SIM-buhl)—a design or an object that stands for something else

tax (TAX)—money that people or businesses must give to the government to pay for what the government does

World Heritage site (WURLD HAIR-uh-tij site)—an area or structure chosen and protected by the United Nations Educational, Scientific, and Cultural Organization for its importance to the world

Read More

Huddleston, Emma. *Exploring Independence Hall.* Lake Elmo, MN: Focus Readers, 2020.

Hurt, Avery Elizabeth. *The Declaration of Independence.* New York: Cavendish Square, 2019.

Murray, Laura K. *The Declaration of Independence.* North Mankato, MN: Capstone, 2020.

Internet Sites

Independence Hall
https://www.nps.gov/inde/learn/historyculture/places-independencehall.htm

Independence Hall
https://www.visitphilly.com/things-to-do/attractions/independence-hall/#must-see

Independence Hall Facts for Kids
https://kids.kiddle.co/Independence_Hall

Index

200th birthday (United States), 22–23

Assembly Room, 18, 27

bell, 10, 23
birthplace of the United States, 15, 22, 28

changes, 18, 20
colonies/colonists, 6, 8, 10, 12–15, 16
Constitutional Convention, 16–17, 27
construction dates, 9, 10
Continental Congress, 13, 15, 16–17

Declaration of Independence, 5, 15, 18, 26
design, 9, 10

governments, 6, 12–13
Great Britain, 6, 12–15

Independence National Historical Park, 24–25

Liberty Bell, 23
location, 5, 8

Philadelphia, Pennsylvania, 5, 6, 8, 15, 22

Revolutionary War, 14, 16, 18

taxes, 12

U.S. Constitution, 17, 18, 26

wings, 9, 20
World Heritage site, 28